The Heirs to t[...]
Three foster sisters [...]
inherited ranch a home.

"Why don't you save us both a bunch of trouble and admit how you feel about me, Zoe?" Ty asked.

She managed a laugh. "It's not flattering."

That infuriatingly sexy smile of his stayed put. "You're crazy about me."

"Crazy, definitely." Zoe flipped her precarious ponytail back, using annoyance to cover her fear. Had she given herself away? He couldn't have guessed her deepest, darkest, most secret fantasy, could he?

Her secret little hope that someday *he* would be the crazy one. *Crazy for her.* Not for the land, but *her.*

Dear Reader,

It's summertime. The mercury's rising, and so is the excitement level here at Silhouette Intimate Moments. Whatever you're looking for—a family story, suspense and intrigue, or love with a ranchin' man—we've got it for you in our lineup this month.

Beverly Barton starts things off with another installment in her fabulous miniseries THE PROTECTORS. *Keeping Annie Safe* will *not* cool you off, I'm afraid! Merline Lovelace is back with *A Man of His Word,* part of her MEN OF THE BAR H miniseries, while award winner Ingrid Weaver checks in with *What the Baby Knew.* If it's edge-of-your-seat suspense you're looking for, pick up the latest from Sally Tyler Hayes, *Spies, Lies and Lovers.* *The Rancher's Surrender* is the latest from fresh new talent Jill Shalvis, while Shelley Cooper makes her second appearance with *Guardian Groom.*

You won't want to miss a single one of these fabulous novels, or any of the books we'll be bringing you in months to come. For guaranteed great reading, come to Silhouette Intimate Moments, where passion and excitement go hand in hand.

Enjoy!

Yours,

Leslie J. Wainger
Executive Senior Editor

Please address questions and book requests to:
Silhouette Reader Service
U.S.: 3010 Walden Ave., P.O. Box 1325, Buffalo, NY 14269
Canadian: P.O. Box 609, Fort Erie, Ont. L2A 5X3